The Poet and His Shadow

by

CIARAN O'DRISCOLL

DEDALUS

The Dedalus Press
24 The Heath, Cypress Downs, Dublin 6W, Ireland.

ISBN 0 948268 72 7 (paper)
ISBN 0 948268 73 5 (bound)

Cover design and painting: Siobhan Piercy

Printed by The Nationalist, Carlow.

Acknowledgement is due to the editors of the following publications in which some of these poems previously appeared: *Ambit, Cyphers, The North Dakota Quarterly, Orbis, The Poetry Ireland Review, Poets Aloud Abu 1988, The Salmon, The Simon Anthology of Poetry,* "Writing in the West" *(The Connacht Tribune).*

The Dedalus Press receives financial assistance from An Chomhairle Ealaíon, The Arts Council, Ireland.

Dedalus Press

John F. Deane

COMHAIRLE CHONTAE ÁTHA CLIATH THEAS
SOUTH DUBLIN COUNTY LIBRARIES

LUCAN LIBRARY
TO RENEW ANY ITEM TEL:

Items should be returned on or before the last date below. Fines, as displayed in the Library, will be charged on overdue items.

CONTENTS

A man who is possessed by his own shadow is always standing in his own light and falling into his own traps. Wherever possible, he prefers to make an unfavourable impression on others. In the long run luck is always against him, because he is living below his own level and at best only attains what does not suit him. And if there is no doorstep for him to stumble over, he manufactures one for himself and then fondly believes he has done something useful.......

.......the shadow, although by definition a negative figure, sometimes has certain clearly discernible traits which point to a quite different background. It is as though he were hiding meaningful contents behind an unprepossessing exterior. Experience confirms this; and what is more important, the things that are hidden usually consist of increasingly numinous figures.

C.G.Jung, *Four Archetypes*

IN BROAD DAYLIGHT...

A swollen stream is wearing away
the sides of the earth, snow has segmented the hills,
and the sky has taken me unawares
with inappropriate total blue. Ice
is melting from a roof of uneven
slates, and there's a glare on walls
of pebble-dashed whiteness. The scene
is set for panic in broad daylight.

It seems I am not yet entirely
a friend to myself; something without a home
or name, grown tired of the old placebos,
has blown its cover and begun to scream.
Around the side of the house, I'm terrified
by the lean cats coming out of their winter shed.

THE FIELD-WATCHER

At the end of another working day,
that thin crop of grass speckled with hawkbit
has lured him along the river pathway
to stand and look, beside the rusted gate.

He admires the field's peculiar features:
its humps and flatnesses; the extinct puddle
of a hollow ringed with broadleaved rushes;
the flowering stump of elder near the middle.

And at the far end, where a wooded clump
rises with a sense of shadows and boundaries,
he sees the horse's elevated rump
and grazing head under the trees.

EVERGREENS

Standing shoulder to shoulder
inside a low stone wall,
dumbfounded witnesses
who will never leave this scene,

they are looking inwards, inwards
at some event or disaster,
with their backs to a man approaching
inquisitively from the road.

And lifting aside a drape
of sharp incense, he also looks
inwards, hoping to find
a place of rest and headstones,

but sees a spotted dog instead,
alert and sniffing the air
on the arched veranda
of a graceless suburban house

and he is forever stunned
into a tough wood and his dark
overcoat is turned
into a tweed of evergreen.

NIGHT PORTER

Chiselled in black, a lioness
couchant on both sides of the staircase
neither keeps watch nor falls asleep.

The night porter conspires to keep
the obsequies of a gangster from eyes
under a dome window of stained glass
in motifs of flowers and fruit,
from guests who are sitting down to eat
a sea-bed served on ice. Platefuls
of empty crustacean shells
are carefully removed by waiters.

Meanwhile, the pensive night porter
is interrupted in his trains
of thought to phone an ambulance
for a call girl injured in bondage,
to go upstairs and disengage
young lovers who sneaked to a room.

The dancers are leaving the ballroom,
the lobby brightens with evening dress.

The night porter's face is expressionless.

PROMISED LAND

Midmorning in the street, a traveller boy
hoarsely revamps a song too often heard,
pocketing infrequent coins of pity
as they drop in his tray of aeroboard.

Unlike the Israelites in the desert,
who worshipped the works of their own hands,
the designers of plastic awnings
on several nearby restaurants

will dine elsewhere this evening. Right now
they are travelling back through history
in a russet sea of marshgrass parted
by the Aaron's rod of the railway.

FAT MAN, SWEEPING

He keeps his secrets, the man who appears
on the rim of my world in a halt of traffic —
a fat man in white shorts and T-shirt
who sweeps the steps of a guesthouse and casts
a few proprietorial glances
over the rim of his own world into
a morning of countless activities
and trades. With an abrasive power tool,
a young man in the nextdoor garden strips
discoloured paint from ornamental railings.
Hundreds are walking, hundreds caught like me
in the traffic's temporary stasis,
and into this desultory moment
a thin rumour insinuates itself
of an infinitude of lives beyond me.
A few last casual flicks of the brush,
a final viewing of his boundaries,
and already the fat man has moved indoors,
keeping his secrets as the lights turn green.

THE SEA AND THE RETIRED CLERK

An inlander who remembered hearing
the sea was the place for the breath of life,
I take the air between lunch and dinner,
whitehaired and cautious in a raincoat.

Especially when the light is hesitant,
I look at the colours in a folding wave —
cloudier than champagne, not quite
the brown and green translucence of a grape:
by God, what a job for a scant palette
of primary colours, raw materials!

Everything seems to be moving, flowing
from itself into everything else
and back again in the soft flap of the breeze:
seaweed and sand, rockpools, cloud-shadows,
even cormorants drying their spread wings!

A far cry from the cobwebbed analecta,
the yawning wisdom of my office days,
in the ozone of continued existence,
I walk the beach, working up an appetite.

CINECAMERA, 1944

It's a dream war, silent,
and in colour for the first time.

Revisited after four years,
France is still green, in Kodachrome.

Behindhand, as in dreams,
we arrive at collapsed towns —
our jeep had its windows polished
a few feet earlier —

and here's a garrotted German,
green as his trenchcoat,
in the gutter as we pass,

and viridescent tints
of prisoners darting unpractised smiles
as they clamber on backs of trucks.

Except for a desert-brown fox —
de Gaulle taking the salute in Paris —
everything in the slow Allied
advance has a green bias,

until winter sets in
with snowdrifts, trenchfoot,
and a brief stalemate.

A HOBO ON THE IMAGINATION

Such a great gift is the imagination
in the gutters of railway stations
and in gutters everywhere,
by hackneyed foul canals
and on clichés of park benches,
searching, not for the *mot juste*,
but for dry newspapers at the end of day,

that can dream lakes of flamingoes
with almost-scented tints
while express trains in the night
scream by like razor blades,
but cannot bring itself to say
this happened me because
I had no market price.

Such a great gift is the imagination
that can tear parrots apart with its hands
and terriers and their owners
as they wait aimlessly for trains
in the arse pockets of railway junctions
where it keeps its Ph.D.s
from penniless universities.

HOME

In the suburbs, nothing happens
in the nicest way: I listen
to the clock, a politician
refusing to speculate beyond
the dozen hours that are in hand.

Small tigers sleep in a jungle-memory
of potted plants, and the sky
outside is blue and clear
between showers in October.

Who knows? Perhaps from now
to twenty years from now
I'll be untroubled by
the long shudder of history.

I share with the nine lives of the cats
a disappointment every time
I'm brushed off trying to climb
on the lap of what I imagine is
possible other than this —

nothing to write home about,
a home, the walls of a house,
a window looking out
on a vista of more houses,
a road that runs
to the hiatus of middle distance
between the town and the hills.

WINTER

The year has outlived its soul-searching brightness;
suddenly in November I'm aware
of a mute countryside in early darkness
outside the angled suburban shadows,

and something has taken root in me
that finds a mirror image in creatures
lacking internal light, in textures
denser than dreamless sleep.

Half-forms of nostalgia and hibernation
have returned to their own like ghosts
I thought had been well and truly laid,
dead game on a scullery wall.

TO BARCELONA AND BACK, 1963

"Oui, monsieur, qu'est-ce que vous desirez?"
enquired the camping site director
with the bored look of a graduate
sunken beneath his metier.

I forget what I was looking for —
I wasn't polite enough then
to *desire* things, I was trying
to equal the other hard men

in a Volkswagen minibus
who stole souvenirs from restaurants
and bales of straw to ease their bones
on the baked earth of the South of France.

In Lloret de Mar and Tossa de Mar,
I had English breakfasts in small hotels,
wearing the stripteaser's straw hat
I stole from a nightclub in Pigalle.

When someone refused to pay for drinks,
a row broke out in a taberna,
but a timely peacemaker called it
a "differencia de costumbre".

The contents of a chamber pot
were thrown from a window on a plaza
where we played toreros in the hours
after the "hasta mañana".

We had fried potatoes in their skins
with steak and beer made of chemicals
beside the Mediterranean.
A beautiful girl in a brothel

on a rambla of Barcelona
took me on her knee but not to bed,
and nothing compared with waking
at dawn in a Normandy hayshed

with the road stretching before you,
though I lived on a meal of egg and chips
a day when the money ran low
and we drove almost non-stop

back into France, through mountains
where "oeuf" had a different ring,
through Clermont Ferrand and Moulins
to a last Parisian fling.

I had nothing to hide from customs,
disembarking at Dun Laoire,
only a green-shrouded corn-cob,
the winter-feed of memory.

A VETERAN RECALLS THE TROJAN WAR

First there was a case of abduction, then
a prolonged siege, and finally the Horse.

And *that* was fashioned from our wit's end —
and all because Menelaus wanted
his Helen back — though at that stage
you might say an element of pride
had entered into it: when you spend
the best ten years of your life besieging
a place, you want to see it through.

And why, you may ask, didn't we think
of the Horse before? The answer, of course,
is that to fashion such a Horse
you *have* to be at your wit's end:
you're no longer going through the motions
like a common or garden besieger
who follows the handbook because
he's not paid to do anything better.

After ten years, when you face
the prospect of returning home
with nothing to show the folks except a few
trinkets, shields and shrunken heads,
then you begin to rack your brains.

SMOKE WITHOUT FIRE

"I see smoke without fire," declared
the old man in the flapping tent,
"but when the thickening smoke will stand
aside for flame I cannot say.

"It has happened many times before
that I have suffered needlessly
from expectation when the sky
grew dark with smoky messengers.

"Smoke has set me apart
and sent me to live on this hill.
I am punished for smoke like a child
who cannot build a fire.

"Down in the kraal, where things have stayed
as they were in the beginning,
dogs bark when I beg for bread,
smoke-alarms blink in taverns."

Thus cryptically spoke
the old man in the flapping tent
who could not make the future flame
when he stood aside from the present.

TOUR DE FRANCE

On one amazing afternoon that July,
when we were walking between fields
of sunflowers, arguing the toss
about dope-testing in the Tour de France,
Marie kicked off her awkward black high heels
and lay in her tight skirt in the grass.

For hours my head was in her frizzled hair
of caramel, my hands were on her breasts
while a hundred cyclists climbed the Alpe d'Huez,
competing like shadows for the substance
of the yellow jersey or failing that
the combined, the red, the green, the polka dot.

Somehow I knew I'd never stick the pace
from argument to ecstasy,
and once I almost prayed she'd miss the train,
stepping down to pick some plums that leaned
over the tiny platform's fence
at a whistle-stop somewhere in Burgundy.

Was it Planckaert or Sean Kelly wore
the green jersey that year?
My favourite colours were combined:
a green T-shirt to match green eyes
and a suit the colour of Spanish tiles
to match her point-scoring lipsticked mouth.

But the agony and jubilation
of heaving to those polka-dotted heights
exacted their anticipated price
in the all-important matter of G.C.:
I began to lose my ground, and Marie gained
the yellow jersey of antipathy

after a contretemps about the scant
press coverage of the Women's Tour.
She was in Paris weeks ahead of me.
Now I remember her with the scent
of green yellowing apples littered on
a tiny platform in Burgundy.

CARING VERSE

It is the earnest desire of this verse
to have an end with football hooligans,
to prevent forever the rampages
of yobboes through the quiet pentameters
of Saturday afternoons and find a garden
running down to the bank of a river
where a long-drawn-out stillness will impinge
eventually on every sense and desire,
a place without television or radio
bearing Greek gifts of facts and figures.

It is my contradictory desire
in this caring verse to keep the patios
of suburbia intact from rows on rows
of impinging Coronation Streets,
to set up home a century from where
I recommend the rope for football louts,
to return to a recognizable
aesthetic of water-dipping branches
each evening, leaving my murals
of killing fields to the public galleries.

SUNSETS AND HERNIAS

They don't have hernias about boiling
lobsters alive: they haven't got the lobsters.
They don't have hernias about the colours
of sunsets — cinnamons, wines and lemons —
because they can't put names on what they see,
and anyway, they haven't got the time
to look, too busy mopping hotel floors,
washing stacks of dishes, looting dustbins.

They don't drown *angst* in hundred-year-old brandies,
and they can't drown their anger in flat beer.
Since sickness means the loss of pay, they save
their hernias as long as they are able,
and can't afford to spend them on the thoughts
of lobsters boiled alive or colours they can't name.

THE TRAGEDY OF CATS
(i.m. Steve Biko)

What is this look the cat is giving me
as I stroke him along the spinal cord
and tell him Steve Biko is dead?

The tragedy of cats is fear, not hope:
one night we found the other cat halfway
up the back door, clinging to the key,
staring in terror at the washing machine
in the paroxysm of its final spin.

"It's our country, man. We travel where we like."
I stroke the cat along the spinal cord
and tell him Steve Biko is dead,
feeling the bone and life beneath
the tiger stripes of his well-fed pelt,

fascinated by the darkness behind
the vesical pupils of his eyes.

THE POET AND HIS SHADOW

Finding that certain inner resources
were no longer accessible to him,
he claimed it was because his shadow
always got in his light. This happened
especially when he reached with the tongs
into the coal bucket beside the fire.
He'd say he was a poet, not a stoker.

His shadow also got in his light
in his roles of dish-washer and cat-feeder,
though he managed to cook a tolerable meal
whenever his shadow stood beside him,
handing him oregano and paprika.

All this had nothing to do with the way
his rooms were facing — it happened
in every house he lived in and at night.
So he put an ad in a magazine:
"Wanted. Shadow that will not stand
in the light of potential poet
in exchange for shadow, excellent cook."
Strangely, although the world is full
of shadows, not one of them answered;
the phone hung silent for twenty years.

And then one day he saw an ad
in a local paper: "Shadow Trainer.
Guaranteed to train personal shadow
to stand behind the light in three weeks
or money back." So he took his shadow
to the shadow trainer and after three weeks
and many years of litigation had
his money refunded.

Must he now be
content to stoke the fire with lumps of coal
he never chooses but are hit upon
by a tongs in the hand of a blind man?
To write poems no one will read
because of the shadow on them and in
between times wash invisible
dishes and feed imperceptible cats?

A snowman is a representation
of a man, and the shadow that it casts
is the shadow of a shadow. The sun
melts both snowman and shadow — and this image
is itself a shadow of death
which guarantees instantaneous darkness
and never promises money back.

ICARUS

Something, perhaps no more
than a rumour of chemistry,
remains from the night they bonded
in crystals of tenderness.

The guy was hooked on flying,
but soon the ferocious fire
of boredom in her eyes
melted the days and nights congealed
in his energetic wings.

Hot wax scalded
his skin in the descent
to an expanse of ocean —
her enormous hungover yawn,
with the clashing rocks of her teeth
and not a rescue craft in sight.

Falling, he glimpsed the child —
a peasant driving horse and plough
around a hump of field
on the headland's wall of death.

ROONEY'S MOUTH

Rooney, the cat, has swallowed my past
and is sleeping it off on the sofa.
I'd like to recover a few small pieces
before digestion begins in earnest,
but I baulk at the thought of explaining
a disembowelled cat when my wife comes home.

A different theory says that I should comb
the Dock Road in our red Sentra tonight,
since all the other women I've ever loved
have become prostitutes from sheer despair
of realizing what they lost in me.

And through the mornings and afternoons,
they sleep in wretched bedsitters, watched over
by the Sacred Heart and his perpetual lamp,
courtesy of pious but unsuspecting
landladies who won't mend their leaking roofs.

There's one piece of the very recent past
I'm so insanely hooked on, I'm afraid
the sofa may be shortly soaked in blood.
I can't think of a plausible excuse
to visit the Dock Road tonight:

the famous fishmonger closed at five,
and smoked salmon and lobsters crammed in tanks
so tightly they have scarcely room to writhe
and prove to customers they're still alive
and shelled prawns and fillets of hake and sidelines
in woodcock and grouse fell into Rooney's Mouth.

CRUTCHES

1. *Crutches*

The word, that used walk round on crutches,
has gone automatic: you can summon it
in stupendous quantities at the press
of a button, the jiggle of a mouse.
Its former crutches will now be raffled
as *objets d'art* to buy a word-processor
for another prolific but crippled
child of genius: these are the famous crutches
that supported the *mot juste* when it came
limping onto a page out of the forest
of the dead of night and Baudelaire's
sept vieillards when they came out of the mist
of a Paris morning, each one but the leader
blind with a hand on his predecessor's shoulder.

2. A Different Weather

A blanket of November haze-weather
has caused the distant hills to disappear.
Over the table of the drab district
the roofs are cards a child has stacked in pairs.

Nothing, it seems, will lift my animal
spirits: this is a weather that's a horse
of a different colour from any other,
and nothing moves in this colourless horse.

In this statuesque emptiness, not even
the smell of sweat or droppings stirs,
but the nostrils are teased unpleasantly
by a miserable coldness that prefers

hoarding its few tight-fisted coins
to spending them for love of ice or sun.

3. Midas

My stomach churning from the heave of ocean,
I have dropped anchor in suburbia,
becoming a Midas of irony
under my battened hatches late at night
when everything I touch turns ludicrous —
music-hall dancers in top hats and tails
that won't bear scrutiny in cold daylight,
waltzing their way into a baton charge.

What do I stand for when the chips are down?
Jobs for the jobless, homes for the homeless?
Yes, but I end up in the murk and shadows
of the harbour and its environs, chasing
the girl with the too-malleable smile
who hates the kitsch upholstery of my cabin.

4. *Threads*

On a bright autumn morning at the corner
of Mallow Street and Pery Square,
I'm listening to a friend unravelling threads
of a spy trilogy he's lately read.
His son beside us is abstractedly
shining a chestnut from the People's Park
on the sleeve of his pullover. My car
is waiting in the cold and dark
of a street that never gets the morning light.
I'm listening to these ins and outs
of double-dealing and conspiracy
because the sun is shining on this corner,
improbable as a cheerful chapter
opened at random in the book of history.

THE ISLAND

Worn to tatters at the end of day
in this haven of peace without goodwill,
I am content to look and listen while
three men describe their trek from peace to force
by way of Sharpeville or Soweto,
becoming as the credits slowly rise
shy singers of a chant of Africa.

And I remember something of myself
in the sense of proud success one of them said
endurance of imprisonment can give,
but for me it was a sense of shamed defeat
in a little Robben Island of the mind
I've never really left although I left
priesthood and monastery years ago.

My priestly mentors, sunk in holy sloth,
a passive cult of God's inscrutable will,
accepted everything and did nothing,
and in that *laissez-faire* I came to think
human with human talents valueless,
blinded like many others by the smokescreen
in which the few escape to privilege.

Things are no better in society.
Unlike the singers of Azania,
I bring my prison with me to this day:
the tide lays bare the foreshore of ill-will
where I am neutralized and pacified,
a beachcomber in need of violence
against this island-fortress of despair.

MEETING NOWHERE

I remember holding on to a wall
for dear life, and one thing that didn't phase
as my fingers slipped from the grainy crevices —
the will to live. Below me, the city
was an immense gasworks of bad vibes,
and the people in the house I had escaped from
were puncturing my effigy with needles.
An unspeakable chant was in my ears,
reducing the time-bubble I lived in,
my *vesica piscis*, to the size
of a cat's pupil in midsummer sun,
suffocating, crushing me between
the convex and concave polarities.
Inwards and outwards was all of one piece,
a world returned to its *materia*
prima — unknowable, unloveable.
Conspiracy had put the squeeze on me:
I staggered backwards and fell on the snow.

I could fable what I experienced then
as hearing a tree barking while it strained
on the dog-chain of its limitations
and pulped itself into a treatise
on existential *angst;* or meeting a fish
at midnight on a deserted road
when the stars were closing down, and thinking "This
is not only not flesh, it's unthinkable."

When I recovered, there were two young men
standing in the porch-light of the house.
I could hear them talking about poetry,
and one was wrapping a scarf around his neck.
"It's as if I don't exist", I thought,
and was afraid to return into the light
in case they couldn't see me or — worse still —
that the one heading home would walk through me.

JACOB

He handled the great disaster
craftily, with kid gloves,
distributing lentil soup wherever
the starving had birthrights to sell.

He had ways of making you talk:
industrial secrets, indiscretions
of ministers danced like meadows in
his breeze; the government fell.

Later, it seems, he ran up against
a ladder that knocked sense into him,
and a strange business dislocated his hip.

His enemies were mollified
by the general amnesty; he launched
a massive poverty programme.

THE GARDEN OF POSSIBLE FUTURES

In the garden of possible futures,
there's no question of profundity
or guilt in the broadest sense,
though there may be some reason
why the gardener sprinkles his boots.

While Catriona phones for a taxi,
a languor of plums and peaches
wounds the heart of a great angler
who crucially lacks assertiveness,

a great angler of plums and peaches
who sprinkles his boots in the depths
of the garden of possible futures.

While Catriona waits for a taxi,
her father, another great angler,
a motionless pike in the drawing room,
will drink a post-prandial brandy.

No question here of profundity
or guilt in the broadest sense.
In the depths of the garden of possible futures,
Catriona hears lullabies in her nightmares.

THE ANARCHIST

The fifty-odd parts of myself
I succeeded in pulling together
from their conflicting schedules
in the supreme effort of expression
produced this painting of an anarchist
waiting for a train at a country station.

As the critic who conducted
the orchestra of gasps and sighs
at my first exhibition said,
it is delightfully inauthentic —
that figure in the foreground
beneath a sign for London trains

who faces straight out of the picture,
the collar of his black overcoat
turned up, his eyes hidden
by the rim of a black hat,
the stray mongrel on the left
clearly cringing away from him.

You can see the smoke in the distance
and across the tracks, on the other platform,
a woman with a parasol
wearing a bustled dress
and a porter beside a wheelbarrow
kneeling to tend the flower-bed.

A moment arrested in time,
as the critic said, the tranquil everyday
separated by railway lines
from a latter-day Dick Whittington,
though the bulge in his overcoat pocket
certainly isn't a cat.

LITTLE OLD LADIES

Adept at the furtive knee in the groin
and the elbow in the solar plexus,
little old ladies jump the bus queue
waving their out-of-date passes.

On the 16.40 to Raheen,
foraging gangs of three or four
little old ladies surround the conductor
and tell him to stick his peak-hour fare.

Little old ladies conspire to bring
the economy crashing down
by blocking supermarket checkouts
and driving weekend shoppers insane

with an endless supply of pennies counted
out of their moth-eaten purses.
Little old ladies spend their pensions
on knuckledusters and karate courses.

Little old ladies read poems, my foot!
The little old ladies I have seen
on the 16.40 to Raheen
were leafing through manuals of guerilla warfare

and would spit on the *Penguin Book of Contemporary Verse.*
I have seen grown men break down and cry
on the 16.40 to Raheen
when fixed by a little old lady's eye.

DAYS OF MAY, 1988

The time of year I have been waiting for
arrives like a great standstill or full stop:
although the whitethorn blossom runs amok
in the fields of Dooradoyle once more,
I have no summer sentiments prepared
due to the non-fruition of my hopes.

As if going about his daily business,
everyone is quietly packing his car,
and a world made fit for heroes has become,
once more, a world without heroes: a kind
of post-survival dust has settled on
the twentieth century's suburbs of farewell.

My love, from the window at which I still
sit fast, having nowhere else to go
and knowing no other life than this one in
the dream city of justice and goodwill,
I watch the distant hills grow migrant-dark
and know there's only a few of us left.

MY FATHER'S GARDEN

In my father's garden there are many stalks,
a little forest of green jesters
with white and yellow flowers for cap and bells,
and my father has sworn allegiance
to this staple of the dispossessed,
declaring that he'd "die for a potato",
and also to their pillow-talk in taverns —
his neck her pillow on a market day.

And there's a poster in the sub post office
of an enormous Colorado beetle,
a black destroyer on a yellow ground,
and after planting-time my father dreams
a whole nation of them are subdividing
tenancies in his drills, and that his green
jesters are shrivelling potato-stalks,
and the *spéirbhean* of his poetry is *The Scream*.

Grim and disillusioned, my father digs
and lifts — clay crumbles from the fork —
healthy pink potatoes are kissed by light
as if to make amends too late
for all that pother about a tuber:
Brittania's trident of *laissez-faire*
points corn and livestock to the export road,
Victoria has a tear in either eye.

SHADOWSPEAK

From that first instance of your panic,
in broad daylight, when I felt called upon
to scream beside you silently,
I have been with you to this moment,
plaguing you with that lack of definition
which was almost, at times, your comfort.
It was my business to be projected
before you, behind you, or beside you;
but sometimes, though you didn't know it,
I wandered to the far end of a field
where I mingled with woodland shadows
or to the far side of a road or street,
becoming a street singer or a man
turned evergreen from bearing witness.
I was a night porter weary with secrets
of corruption, a fat man sweeping steps,
a retired clerk taking the sea air,
a garrotted German in a green trenchcoat.
I was the hobo, imagination:
if you looked hard enough, you'd have seen me
in the *vesica piscis* of the cat's eye.
When I'd tiptoe up behind you on returning
from a wander in the redolent woods
of memory, I'd notice how
you shivered, sensing presences
that trailed me back: half-creatures sniffing at
the curious present — ghosts of dead game
in your grandmother's scullery, a girl
you met in a Barcelona brothel.

Being your lack of completeness, I am
both past and future: a veteran
recalling the trojan horse of history,
and a smoky seer who cannot coax
the future into flame. I am poetry,
mingling, in the nature of shadows,
with other shadows, walking through them,
confusing love affairs with cycle races,
pentameters with football hooligans.
And even then I'm only halfway through
my repertoire: the hardest acts ensue.

As if a stone impacted in a duct
of flesh and blood could turn my shadow-skin
a jaundiced olive green, I've lived
too long with the resentment of the poor,
a sickness that can't pay for medicine,
and hereby warn you I'll no longer be
your lack of definition in that sense —
a cat-stroking suburban moralist,
a smoke-blinded reformer in an armchair.
No one believes that yarn about *my* getting
in *your* way; but people would rather like
to know how often *you* have got in *mine*.
Soon you may take the plunge like Icarus,
dragging me with you into Rooney's Mouth,
and I've no wish to end my shadow-days
a cripple limping in colourless weather,
playing lockjaw to a tetanus
of economic greed and misery;
a protest marcher in top hat and tails
tap-dancing between teargas cannisters;
or like the shadow of your artist friend,
the trilogy-unraveller who's been sent
to prison for the non-payment of debts
while you armchair on *angst* and history!

Speaking of prison, I've served my time
in the tiny Robben Island of your mind.
And just as you became a shadow briefly
on a winter's night in Cork, I'd like to try
my hand at being substance for a change.
Unless, that is, *you* change: go knock your head
on some benevolent ladder; otherwise
this is our garden of the forking paths.
Who knows? Perhaps like my ancestor in
Andersen's tale, I'll enter government;
or failing that, depending on my sex,
become a latter-day Dick Whittington
or a little old lady running amok
in crowded supermarkets and buses
like hawthorn through the fields of Dooradoyle.
Already I grow restless at your feet,
a jester tugging at these tuberous roots.

EPILOGUE: THE SHADOW-CAT

The cat sits on the ledge inside the window
and watches me returning through the dusk.
Predictable as the hands of a clock,
the eyes of the cat are on my return.
Behind the cat, a fire has just been lit.

I fix myself a quick identity
relating to these three — dusk, fire and cat:
a man a cat is watching in the dusk
watching a cat in the glow of a fire.

The dusk is snowflakes falling in the deep.
A shadow at its heart consumes the fire.
The cat's a shadow-cat, an edgeless blur.

Run to me, love, when I open the door,
and hold me as you do falling asleep.